3 R'S

REFLECTION

Recovery

REDEMPTION

ANNETTA M. WILLIAMS

3 R'S

REFLECTION RECOVERY REDEMPTION

By ANNETTA M. WILLIAMS

Published by One Faith Publishing

Richmond, VA

onefaithpublishings@gmail.com

This book or parts thereof may not be reproduced in any form, stored in a retrieval system, or transmitted in any forms by any means--electronic, mechanical, photocopy, recording, or otherwise-- without written permission of the publisher and/or author, Annetta M. Williams, except as provided by United States of America copyright law.

Unless otherwise noted all Scripture quotations are from the King James Version (KJV) used by permission of public domain.

Copyright © 2020 by Annetta M. Williams

All rights reserved.

Table of Contents

Acknowledgments 1

Forword 8

Introduction. 11

Chapter One: Being an Overcomer 13

Chapter Two: Facing My Fears 28

Chapter Three: Hurt People Hurt People 41

Chapter Four: A Godly Woman with a Purpose 53

Chapter Five: A Godly Woman 63

Chapter Six: Woman build your Faith, You will overcome doubt 68

About The Author 80

Acknowledgments

I acknowledge and thank God for my beautiful children. My mother, Daisy Kirkwood-Jackson has displayed the strength of a warrior even when she did not know it was in her. My dad, Ben Rosenthal, saw and believed I have the ability and talent to do a multitude of things, and he proudly supports them all.

Also, a special thanks to my sisters because you inspired me to write this book.

A special thanks to my dear sister-in-law, Barbara Hargrove, and Chettie Martin; we have a relationship like Naomi and Ruth. She will never leave me, and I will never leave her.

To my dear beloved brothers.

To the anointed, appointed, and appreciated man of God, Pastor William Gillison, my pastor, whom I can proudly say is a true man of God who is walking in a burst of faith. God has allowed Pastor Gillison to be a father figure as well as an encourager of my God-given abilities. Pastor Gillison was also the one who inspired the chapter, "Hurt People Hurt Others".

One day in June of 2007 my pastor spoke to me on the phone and called that spirit right out: "You hurt, so you hurt others." Praise God because on that day my breakthrough began.

A Special Word from Pastor Charles McCarley

"I am redeemed, bought with a price; Jesus has changed my whole life. If anybody asks you just who I am, tell them I am redeemed." –Jessy Dixon

Minister Annetta Williams's publication of **Reflection, Recovery, and Redemption** is an on-time review of what people can and should strive for in everyday life. This book, though born out of personal struggles and triumphs, will help the reader in navigating through their own various plights of life. We are all aware of the struggles that life may bring, but I am reminded of a scripture within the Bible that says in Revelation 12:11, "And they overcame him by the blood of the Lamb, and by **the word of their testimony**."

You are an overcomer when you learn how to release and face issues head-on. Many will find healing from the words that we keep locked up; this book, so wonderfully authored, will give us insight on the power of our testimony; the life story that's within us deserves a voice.

Minister Annetta has poured her soul into this publication, and with decades of experience both natural and spiritual, I have no doubt that this book will provide a plethora of principles and strategies for you, beloved, to be able to process through anything that comes your way in life.

Being a leader in the Lord's church, I encounter on numerous occasions those who simply need guidance in their daily walk; oftentimes my response is that you simply need a mentor, someone who has already been where you are trying to go.

It's my experience that often the change that we seek is within us, but there's no person (mentor) to stir the greatness that lies dormant within. This book shall challenge you, encourage you, as well as cause you even to shed a tear, but it is designed to stir the greatness that's within you, reduce your pride, and eliminate fear, so the many that are dealing with the same issues can find levels of peace in their own storms.

May I leave you with this thought: there is a particular story written within the Bible located in the book of Ruth, and yes, it's a very familiar story that many already know, so I will jump to the key point here. Ruth eventually ended up with her husband, Boaz, but it didn't happen right away; she had to endure the process before she was able to obtain the prize. It was her commitment to Naomi that caused her to move strategically and, in the end, gave her a victory.

When you travel through the pages of this book I encourage you to truly listen to the transparency of her heart, for many of us will receive victory if we listen to those who have endured the process; you can overcome depression, you can overcome abuse, you can overcome loneliness, you can overcome anything that comes to challenge your greatness if you place your heart and mind to it. Allow this book to be a part of your Naomi experience, one that will help guide you through the process to a better and greater you.

In my closing (cause yes I am a preacher), the perplexities of life are not greater than the omniscience and omnipotence of our God; our older sainted mothers and fathers of the church would sing a song entitled, **"I am redeemed, bought with a price, Jesus has changed my whole life…"** I want to tell you, beloved, that redemption is nigh; the definition of being redeemed simply means to be delivered or rescued. Many need a rescue; this book throws out a lifeline that will help pull you to shore. Place yourself in the words, understand that you too can be delivered to a greater or higher level of existence. Free yourself from the worry of the various vicissitudes of life and finance; know that there's a greater power that leads and guides you on the daily; He did it for me, He did it for Minister Annetta, and He can do it for you. Blessings to you.

Because of Christ,
Pastor Charles McCarley
Tabernacle of Praise Church, Buffalo, NY

A Special Word from Deirdra Taylor

It takes great courage to pen your life for the world to see. Knowing the greater need is at hand, Annetta Williams has done just that. In order to succeed, we must be able to acknowledge who we are, where we came from, and where we are going. She has skillfully reflected her life's journey within these pages. It is my prayer that her undeniable courage to unfold before us will grant everyone the spiritual push needed for betterment and not self-condemnation.

We can become easily lost in our desires to be valuable to family, friends, and other connections through our spiritual journeys. **Quite often we conform to connect**. Years may pass before we see how far from the mark we have gone in being who God truly wants us to be. Thank you for reminding us to block out the "noise" and focus on God. I am sure there are some parts of this book that will speak directly to your situation as it has mine. This book is a necessary read. It is a great honor to witness the Reflection, Recovery, and Redemption of Annetta Williams!

"For I know the thoughts that I think toward you, saith the Lord, thoughts of peace, and not evil, to give you an expected end." Jeremiah 29:11

My best to you always,

Deirdra Taylor

Forword

Several times over the years, I have listened to my "sister" Minister Annetta Williams ("Netta," as I refer to her), talk about her experiences. Often it was more like "venting" than just sharing a story. She would go on and on about her childhood, her struggles with health issues, her relationships including marriage and relations among members of her family and her children. Often, either of us would conclude by jokingly saying, "This would make a really good book."

After winning a battle with Cancer a few years ago, it seemed the ambition and dream of writing an autobiography or simply telling her life's story became more pressing for her, and she began to ask me for advice and encouragement about how to write her story down.

Like many other people in this world, I myself have faced and overcome some serious struggles during my life, including an auto accident that left me with permanent physical limitations and chronic pain, the death of my younger sibling in 1990 due to senseless violence, and separation and divorce (twice), just to name a few. These experiences and more sharpened my interest in and understanding of what I simply describe as **"LIFE."** But where is real life found? The Bible tells us that we find it abiding in Christ. If we do not abide in Him, we will accomplish nothing. If we abide, seeking first His kingdom in righteousness, then all things we need will be added to us.

The downside to abiding in a rich relationship with God is we are going to have struggles in our lives, but they will strengthen us. As I looked back on how I coped with each of these experiences, I relied on my spiritual faith and someone trustworthy that I could talk or vent with.

Time and time again, I have witnessed Netta overcome challenges and set and achieve goals, including starting a business and building a successful music ministry. So when she sounded serious about writing a book, I advised her to simply *"pray on it, and then tell your story!"*

The result is a very personal story. **My Life & God's Promises - REFLECTION, RECOVERY, REDEMPTION** is not just a story of life and ambition. It is about the family and the childhood that shaped her dreams, about the experiences that sharpened those dreams, and about the struggle to fulfill them. But it is also about some dreams that were nightmares that unfortunately came true and how she learned to live with them, but not just live, but to live abundantly!

Ultimately, it is the story of a strong and determined woman. A woman who lovingly and openly shares her life's stories and the lessons that she learned from them with the hope of helping others to face their realities and allow themselves to be shaped by church, faith, family, and true friends.

In the end, **My Life & God's Promises - REFLECTION, RECOVERY, REDEMPTION** will allow the reader to understand that the product of struggles in life are there to help them get where they are going by remembering where they came from. *REMEMBER - The struggles we meet are meant to strengthen us!* I pray that this book helps you find God's Perfect Peace in the midst of your struggles.

Your brother - Lamont Williams

Introduction

As I struggled preparing this book, I realized that God predestined me to do many things. Still, I could not touch the surface of what He wanted me to do until I surfaced from a place of "Broken to Whole" and "Release for an Increase." One of God's plans for my life is to help restore women who have been deceived into believing that they are everything other than what God has created them to be. A woman's true beauty is a reflection of a Godly Woman just as 1 Timothy 2:9 states:

> *Likewise, I want women to adorn themselves with proper clothing, modestly and discreetly, not with braided hair and gold or pearls or costly garments, but rather by means of good works, as is proper for women making a claim to godliness.*

This scripture is stating that God requires us to be "Likewise" just as He has given to the men to be of good report, then, so shall we. Which means, we must let our works, and what we do for Christ make a volume of praise in our lives while we are on this Christian walk.

> *"Not necessarily the color of her hair, her weight, or the way she dresses, but the awesome way she honors the Lord in her heart and submits her life and ways unto Him (God)."*
>
> *Annetta M. Williams*

Wow, it's amazing how so many people can play a role in the destruction of our lives. But God is so awesome because many played a major role in my destruction, but God has given double for my praise.

As you read this book, some may say she was messed up, and others will say, yes, she was messed up, but she has been placed here to bless others through her testimony. So before you begin reading this book, please pray for an open mind because I would love for you to walk with me on my journey from Self-Destruction to Instruction.

Last but not least, I give Radical Praise to my Father above (God) for allowing my storms to blow through my life. I'm also grateful for God giving me the ability to know that every test does not require a grade but just a Praise. So, in this I'll say, "For God I Live; For God, I Die!"

Chapter One

Being an Overcomer

For whatsoever is born of God overcometh the world: and this is the victory that overcometh the world, even our faith.

Who is he that overcometh the world, but he that believeth that Jesus is the Son of God? 1 John 5:4-5

It's astonishing to see how I am gracefully growing old. I've had so many tragedies occur in my life as a child that I should have lost my mind. Now, I have realized that I went through those things to help build the woman I am today.

So, let's begin…As a child, I grew up in the church. I went to Sunday service, YPWW which was Bible study, and Friday Night Tarry Services. I was churched, but the perplexing part was, all this church, and I was still the worst child. Meaning I was full of anger, hatred, and mischief.

As I reflect on those days, I recall the mothers and missionaries of the church calling the children to the altar on Friday nights to tarry. As I often misbehaved, there were many nights that I stood at the altar rolling my eyes and laughing, and on other occasions, I faked like I passed out just for them to get out of my face.

Throughout my mischievousness, a lady named Mother Lemon repeatedly stated, *"One day you will get saved and get the Holy Ghost."* And one day the inevitable happened: I was around 13 years old when I felt and heard God speak to me for the first time.

During that time of my life, my self-esteem was very low, and I was in the middle of my parents' painful separation. It was at a point in a young girl's life when you need your mother to nurture you even more and for daddy to be your physical shield of protection. In the middle of everything that was already going on, I was experimenting with smoking marijuana and drinking to suppress the emotions of needing to be loved, but regardless of everything that I was going through, I still heard the voice of God on a hot summer day in my uncle's yard. It was a day that I was debating ending my life because I hated myself just that much.

Amid my pain, I cried and asked God,

"Why am I still here?"

And this is when I heard God say, *"I have a purpose for you."*

It was like I was holding a full conversation with God. He continued by saying,

"The purpose in your life cannot be revealed because you will not understand it."

I replied, *"Just tell me what I am living for today?"*

As I waited on God to reply, my mother pulled up in the white church van and yelled, *"Let's go to church!"* and that is when I clearly heard God speak, *"Go to church."* I was extremely confused, but I went anyhow.

On that particular night, the preacher's sermon was about Adam and Eve, but the weirdest part is this: the preacher spoke in the exact voice that I had been hearing all day. The preacher made a statement that I still remember to this day: *"Eve got in God's way with His plan and convinced Adam to follow her lead. Stop trying to follow yourself and follow Me."* As a kid, I didn't quite understand that I had been repeatedly saying to myself, *"Whatever."*

Unfortunately, I left the church that night and turned away from God, and my path of life drastically changed, and it didn't take long before the vindictive Annetta took control. To begin, I started by dating myself. Well, let me explain; as a child, I've seen and lived abusive relationships, so it was only two ways to go: you become the abuser, or you get abused. I chose the greater and became the abuser of myself.

To help suffocate my pain, I turned to sex with boys, and then I moved on to men, just to get what I wanted. Most of the time it was just temporary words to soothe the void of not being loved.

The abuse I gave to men became a game I played with my friends. Our main goal was to see who could get the most men and their attention. My disrespect for men was at an all-time high, and my words became a dangerous weapon. By this time, the drinking and smoking had ceased because I developed a new type of high which was hurting people with words, my actions, and sometimes it was physical harm.

To help occupy my mind, I began spending many hours with my aunt who I fondly called my second mother, and yes, she loved me; I say she loved me because it was out of love that she corrected my wrongs every day. Being around my aunt caused me to slow down with the way I dressed. In that stage of my life, I dressed very provocatively and seductive, and I didn't have a problem with dating older men who were in relationships, but married men were off limits. My philosophy was, *"no commitment;"* this way, I wasn't obligated to see them, and if I did, it was on my time. Truthfully, it never bothered me about hurting women or their families, as long as I was getting my needs met.

As I sought to fill an empty hole, I became obsessed with men, clothes, and jewelry. Outside of the chaos, there were those special moments when my aunt took me shopping and the entire time she would say,

"You don't need no man to have the finer things in life, just want them for yourself, and you can get it."

Two of her famous sayings were,

"Why lay down with a dry behind with nothing, and get up with a wet behind with nothing?"

"Who are you to put a price on your body that doesn't belong to you?"

My story...

The fact that I had been molested, caused me to live several years of my life running from the truth. First, I ran from the reality that I lost something that I never really knew I had. How could I move beyond the fact that someone took it from me? They took away my innocence. An innocence that I was unaware of because I wasn't developed mentally, physically, or emotionally.

Unfortunately, this was my reality, and I wasn't quite sure about what to do with it; therefore, I created a mask to cover the pain and move forward with my life…the problem was, I couldn't run or hide from the pain, yet I kept trying.

I spent years running away while I created more masks to hide behind. The fact was, I longed for something that simply wasn't there. It's like going to the park with the main purpose of getting on the swing but not realizing that everyone else has that same desire. When you get to the park you notice there's a long line of children who also wants to swing, so now you must face the reality that you may not get your chance.

Later in life, I found out that I had to come to grips with these realities and deal with the molestation. I also had to cope with the fact that I had an absent father growing up, a father that I needed so badly…almost as much as I needed air to breathe. But the reality was, I needed to understand by working through the trials, tribulations, hurt, pain, disappointment, disbelief, and the misery of what happened in my life.

Yes, all of those things were my reality, but I masked them by wearing designer clothing, cute shoes, having a great job, etc., but materialistic things could not change the fact that I was broken.

My reality haunted me like night terrors. I was hurt, disappointed, and discouraged, but I kept all of the pain bottled up inside because I was in denial. I became a person that I didn't even know, so every day I struggled as I created someone who didn't exist. I created an image of who I wanted to be from head to toe, including the hair, makeup, and even the clothes. No, it wasn't the real me because I wasn't ready to come face-to-face with my true identity, so I masked any and everything that could reveal the truth.

With each year, I internalized even more, until I finally grew tired and depressed, which led me into creating a new mask. Instead of dealing with reality, I became a victim of my circumstances. I was unaware that I was the victim because I did so well by masking my pain with lies and manipulation…and I believed them all.

I spent some extra time in this chapter so I can share the two main elements of my reality.
First, I refused to face and conquer the truth because of my fears, confusion, and doubt.
Second, I came to understand that the masks I wore did not protect me, my spirit, or my soul, which is my true shields of armor.

Today, I have a greater understanding that the reality of life is not always pleasurable, and it will also place you in the position of a resolution. What I experienced in my earlier years was meant to bend me but not break me. Yes, my experiences caused some damage, but they did not destroy me. I went through some things only so I could know how to become a stronger person while clearly defining who I am and not continuing to allow misery to define my existence.

My reality dictated that I was a child of molestation. For many years I felt as though I did something wrong to be placed in that position, but I learned that position was not my own, yet I was forced into ownership by being violated, and that violation was no longer going to overpower my purpose.

My testimony...

I still remember the pitch-dark room that carried the scent of strong cologne (in my later years I found out it was Old Spice). As I laid still and counted the minutes in my head, time that seemed to be 30 or 40 minutes; yet, it felt like days on days of being touched. But if I told anyone, I could lose everything, probably even my life.

When someone strips away your innocence and makes you feel physically, emotionally, and mentally broken, you don't know what or how to feel. I was a child attempting to live as a child but struggled because I held a nasty secret of no longer being innocent. A secret that produced anger, frustration, bitterness, and betrayal which became a smothering factor for all my realities.

People viewed me as this disrespectful and miserable child, a child that just couldn't tell the truth. But the reality was, I hid my pain by acting out certain behaviors.

I was molested by a family member, but I didn't want anyone to recognize it or know the pain I carried from the ages of nine to fourteen years old. During those years of my life, a lot changed. I didn't trust my ability to be genuine and authentic with people, so the pain caused me not to trust myself or others.

For years I thought I could die any moment, so I became numb to the pain and the thoughts of death, and I just wanted to get away from the reality of being molested. Many may think it's the physical act, but the physical act eventually stops, yet the torment of the actions will follow you for the rest of your life if you don't deal with it openly.

I no longer wanted to be one of his many victims, but how could I truly get to a place of living outside of a victim's shadow? By expressing myself to the individual that caused my pain. I told him how he destroyed the process of my life but not the outcome of my life...

You may have taken my innocence, but you didn't take my identity.

You may have ruined my sexual process to think and embrace a touch, but you have not taken the sense to enjoy what's a genuine expression of seduction and physical contact.

You may have had my mind in a dark cloud, but I stand today knowing the darkest moments in life were there for me to shine brighter.

Now I had to dig deep to forgive him and even deeper to forgive myself for hating myself and everything about me. Now the true healing was able to begin. I reflected and remembered the past and accepted that his faults couldn't continue on my journey of life.

The redemption phase was difficult because he denied the feelings I had, but not the act he performed, stating, "Just let it go and move on." But the reality was, how can I move on if you can't face the truth? Nevertheless, I did because his truth will never be my truth.

Still, I found myself in a battle against myself, 40-year-old Annetta against the 9 to 14-year-old Annetta, and at that point, I began to see my light, and I saw it shining ever so bright.

No longer a victim! Now victorious things are my focal point!
No more holding my mother hostage for not protecting or believing me!
No more not desiring a touch from a man in a true way!
No more dreams of dying slowly because now I just want to live!
I'm an overcomer with Victory!

Studies show there are indisputable long-term negative effects on child sexual abuse for many, if not most, victims. Such problems as eating disorders, substance abuse disorders, and sexual dysfunction, or overly sexual acts.

Some of the most common consequences are guilt, shame, re-victimization, diminished self-esteem, depression, relationship difficulties, and/or other types of dissociative disorders. This does not mean every person who has experienced abuse will necessarily experience symptoms. However, there is an ample amount of evidence that sexual abuse is damaging and warrants intensive and specialized intervention to stop the abuse and bring recovery.

Even some victims may believe they consented because they never told, and that's called abusing oneself. Being asked to participate in activities that are inappropriate for their age/stage of development is a violation of their trust, well-being, and existence.

My Afterthoughts...

It's amazing how we define reality. The majority of our realities is something that we've created in our mind because we tend to block out the negative things that have happened. We find it easier to only think about the things that make us feel good but deny those things that made us feel bad.

We have become conditioned to wearing a mask to cover up the heartache and pain we've experienced. It's like social media…you can only see the highlights of a person's life and not the full reel. We often do this when we are dealing with the reality of our own lives, so we try to forget those hurtful things and move forward. But guess what? You can't.

Our lives are saying to us, "You say you want this? Prove how much. Fight for it. Earn it." Overcoming obstacles is a big part of earning it. There's always going to be resistance, but you'll have to overcome to accomplish anything positive you want to happen. The more tools you have to overcome these forces, the more likely you are able to stay in control and win. Overcoming obstacles in one area gives you the tools for dealing with them in other areas. Listen, my sister,

ANYTHING that you want to do in life will present resistance, but you have to overcome it to make it happen.

Being an Overcomer

"You should never view your challenges as a disadvantage. Instead, it's important for you to understand that your experience facing and overcoming adversity is actually one of your biggest advantages." –Michelle Obama

What obstacles or realties have you faced?

_____

_____

_____

How did you overcome those obstacles?

_____

_____

_____

Chapter Two

Facing My Fears

> *"Be strong and of a good courage, fear not, nor be afraid of them: for the LORD thy God, it is He that doth go with thee; he will not fail thee, nor forsake thee."* Deuteronomy 31:6

The year 1989 is when I began to see life much differently than I had ever seen before; in some odd way, things even felt different. During this season of my life, I was not dating anyone because I experienced a scary moment when I found out that I was pregnant. I really liked this guy, but he was in college doing some great things.

My life took a huge shift on the day I called and told him that I was pregnant, and he replied,

"Are you sure? So what am I supposed to do?" I was devastated by his response, so I hung up the phone.

Overburdened with emotions, I decided to terminate the pregnancy. A few days later he came home for the weekend, and while we sat in his car, he asked me a question, *"What are we going to do?"* At that moment I couldn't give him an answer, so I began to cry because I was too afraid to tell him about what I had done.

As the tears streamed down my face, he comforted me in his arms while reassuring me that he would be in my life forever. At that point, all I could do was weep even more. I vividly remember saying to him, *"You don't deserve me because I don't deserve myself, let alone a baby,"* and that's when I told him about the abortion I received just two days prior. I have never in my life seen a grown man cry; I could feel his broken heart as he cried out the words, *"You didn't even give me a chance to have a part in the decision."*

There were absolutely no excuses for the decision I acted on alone, so I gave him my only reason…I was scared. Keep in mind, this young man was someone who had always been there for me; it didn't matter if it was for family, school, or even other men. Yes, he deserved much more than what I gave, so I listened as his words replayed, *"I should have been there; I'm always by your side."*

Afterward, he took me home, and I went directly to my bedroom, and out of nowhere, I began to feel this warm feeling come over my body. My first thought assumed that it was just the sickness from the procedure, so I rested. Instead of continuing to feel ill, I heard God's voice again: *"You followed Annetta again. You will follow me one day; you have more time."*

All those years I believe that I lived on borrowed time until I recognized who to follow…God. One night while I was at a bowling party with a male friend, a young man asked for my name. I politely responded with an attitude, and in return, he smiled, nodded, and gave me his phone number. A few days later, I was out with a group of friends trying to get into a night club, and there he was again. Initially, my first thought was, oh my, please don't allow this lustful demon to trail me again. Without any hesitation, he said, *"Call me,"* but with my smart mouth I replied, *"No, here's my number; if you want me, call me."*

During the time of our second encounter I was settling down with this one guy, but throughout the entire relationship I saw a different face on him, but I never recognized the face. After the club ordeal, I decided that I was going home for the night, and once I walked through the door, my phone rang. Yes, it was him, and as we conversed, he invited me over for dinner.

Now, this was a first; meaning, most men I dated only wanted one thing, and that was it. In an instant, this man became my rescuer. I had gone through so many things, so he just wanted to keep the focus on getting to know me better, and this is how I began my journey on becoming an overcomer.

This man was not interested in me sexually, and even when I attempted to go further, he replied, *"I want to get into your mind, then I can have your body."* All I could do was laugh, *like yeah,* here goes another line, but he honestly meant that thing. He wasn't like most men; therefore, his uniqueness quickly drew me in. As he reeled me in, my only choice was to block the others out, and with each passing day, we became inseparable.

At the time, I was not attending a church, and neither was he. One day, my beau was invited to attend his friend's church, and because we were a couple, he encouraged me to come along. I was reluctant; reason being, it was Baptist, and I grew up COGIC. Well, we attended, and eventually, he joined the church, and a few months later I also joined. A short timeframe after joining, his whole demeanor began to change. One night out-of-the-blue, he said we have to talk. He proceeded by saying, *"I love you, and I want to marry you."* The funny thing was, he didn't know that all I ever wanted was for a man to say, "I love you," and literally three days later we were married.

Listen, I was married, but I was still a mess as I dealt with the issues from my past and childhood. Yes, we went through many things in our marriage, but we were overcomers. I can truly stand today and say that God uses people to help bring you to a place of awareness in Him. My husband was my beacon of awareness of God's grace in my life. Now, don't misunderstand this: my husband was not the source of my change; he was the very vessel who was used by the Source, which is Jesus Christ.

Ladies, as we go through life, remember the man you are dating may not be the face God has placed in your memory. Meaning, don't settle for less when God can give you the best. We have to wait; as the word of God says, *He that findeth a wife finds a good thing.* Sit still in the process of the cleansing, and allow God to send your husband, and don't follow yourself; follow the path director which is **GOD!** I had to get to God's place in order to realize that He made me special for a divine purpose. I also realized that my life was designed to build me for my future, not as a victim, but as an overcomer.

My Afterthoughts...

An overcomer is a person who was at the point of losing until there was an outlet set before them. An outlet to see that the situation won't kill or fail you but promote you to succeed in every way. As I share my many challenges with you, I pray that you will hear my heart and nothing else.

No, I do not blame or hate men, neither do I blame my past, nor do I wish to have a new nature of understanding. Instead, I can boldly state that I enjoy being the woman who I am today. I have arrived at a place of understanding my role for each day as well as my purpose. Now, I have chosen to share my struggles and obstacles to help push forward purpose-driven women into reaching their full potential. In doing so, each woman will become stronger and blossom into the Godly Woman who has a Purpose and a Plan.

Obstacles are barriers or restrictions that we run into along our life's path. I know in my path, I have become an overcomer from child molestation, sexual abuse to my body, lies, family curses, and many other obstacles that I presented to myself. Some obstacles present themselves as learning experiences, and then we have those obstacles that we jump over, go around, or sometimes knock down, and, finally, there are those rigid obstacles that require a great amount of energy to conquer.

Here are a few of the obstacles that I overcame:

Father Issues

The issue of my childhood disasters, such as the dynamics of my family structure being broken down, and not having a relationship with my father. For most of my life, I hated him for not being what I thought he should have been. Later, this created an unrealistic life and mindset. I forced myself into believing that his absence didn't affect me because I could merely consider him as dead. I recall that if his name came up in a conversation, I quickly responded by saying he was dead. For years, I spoke those words, and many people felt sorry for my loss, but my father's death was an unrealistic illusion that I allowed to be placed inside my head.

Emotional Barriers

I built internal walls to block out my family members, and I set up emotional barriers that prevented anyone from getting too close. Again, this was a disaster from my childhood that I set up. Instead of accepting and dealing with the reality of not having my father, I emotionally detached myself. My emotional detachment affected the way I treated men and what I thought a man desired from me. Those underlying childhood disasters played a huge factor in the latter years of my life.

Submission

The issue of submitting became an obstacle. My first challenge began when I did not fully accept the changes that God had planned for my life. Because I struggled with reality, my submission was unrealistic as well. I was often scrutinized extensively regarding my submissive nature. I was raised in a spiritual family, yet I felt disconnected from my spiritual connection.

Value

I had an issue of not knowing my value. I didn't understand my value or how important I was and am to God. I've always thought less of myself due to not feeling worthy of anything. During this time my world became even more unreal in the way I thought and how I handled my life's concerns, including the make-believe people who I believed loved and cared for me, but those people never existed.

Obstacles became a common practice in my everyday life, to the point that if I wasn't presented with an obstacle my day was not running smoothly. Sadly, obstacles became my everyday…Drama of Life.

My story...

As I matured into a woman and got married, I realized that I was still wearing a mask and running away from my reality. I wanted to escape the in-depth pain I felt in my soul. I believed that if I married at a young age, it would be my underground railroad to freedom from the mental and emotional enslavement of heartache and pain. I wanted an exodus from the empty hole where my happiness was lodged, but I thought that I could find it through the love of an older man.

I lacked the love of my biological father, so I attached myself to a man as I sought to find love through him. I remained in a toxic relationship and marriage because I was looking for a love that my husband wasn't able to give. I desperately wanted him to fill the void of my absent father. I also wanted him to love me unconditionally and make all of the pain go away, but he couldn't do it, nor could he change my past. Instead of relying on him to eliminate the demons that controlled my heart, I was the one who needed to rip off the mask and face my reality. Yet, my marriage became a "fossil" and it was tearing away and breaking down everything that I created and believed was my reality.

I lived in an unrealistic world with unrealistic emotions, and I engaged in unrealistic conversations and made unrealistic decisions. I repeatedly lied to myself and I believed that my life was *good*, my marriage was *good*, and I was *good*, but the reality was…I wasn't.

It wasn't long before I began having seizures, and after visiting the doctor's office on multiple occasions they could not find a diagnosis or a medical reason why I was having seizures. However, the doctors were able to share that I could be having emotional seizures. The doctor asked me if I had ever spoken to a professional about any of the issues that were worrying me. She asked in a way that indicated that surely some things were stressing me out. The doctor asked a question that sparked me to ask myself the following questions:

Had I dealt with my reality?

Had I ever dealt with the situations that happened in my past?

Since I was living in a pretentious world, I denied my questions and all of her questions too, and I simply replied, "*No, there are no issues, nor have there ever been.*" My response was far from the truth; the mask was so thick on my face that it had become a part of who I was.

The reality was, I masked so well that I started to believe that this was the type of life I was supposed to live, and even though each day was a different day, I repeatedly dealt with the same stuff, and every morning I woke up asking myself the same questions:

"Am I really here?"

"Why am I here?"

"What's going on?"

"Is this all real?"

Facing My Fears

"Each of us must confront our own fears, must come face to face with them. How we handle our fears will determine where we go with the rest of our lives. To experience adventure or to be limited by the fear of it." -Judy Blume

What fears have you come face to face with?

_____

_____

_____

How are you transitioning from fearful to victorious?

_____

_____

_____

What are your strengths in the area of fear?

_____

_____

_____

Do you believe your purpose can supersede your fear?

_____

_____

_____

Chapter Three

Hurt People Hurt People

"For I reckon that the sufferings of this present time [are] not worthy [to be compared] with the glory which shall be revealed in us." Romans 8:18

Divorce is like experiencing death because we must go through the grieving process. This process has no time frame attached to it. So don't be deceived by people's words of, *"Get over It!"* or *"It will pass soon."*

But what is soon?

What will Pass?

Those two questions have always stuck out to me until I realized that I must grieve alone. Grieving alone didn't mean God wasn't there; it merely meant I didn't need the interference of another human being. This was the phase in my life that I needed to be alone, so I could embrace and identify with Annetta by accepting my errors and mistakes, along with taking accountability and ownership of my failures. Yes, failures, we all have them, but I have a few questions for you:

- **Do you allow your failures to predicate your future?**
- **Do you cripple yourself along with your emotions?**
- **Do you see beyond the failures and emotions?**

Divorce is a death process and you must grieve through the emotions. I thought that once the divorce papers were signed, everything would be better and I would finally feel relief, but I didn't. Somehow, unexpected emotions of remorse, sadness, and guilt piled on top of bitterness and resentment, and the frustration intensified. My confusion caused me to wonder if I made a mistake, and I began to slowly lose my identity.

I relived my marriage and divorce as I desperately sought answers as to why this happened, what went wrong, and how things could have been dealt with differently. In the back of my mind, I knew the answers, but I was unwilling to accept my fault. I was terrified of judgment from who I thought was my supportive family and friends, so I held it in, and I didn't confide in anyone, especially after trusting many who had no good intentions for me or us.

The solitude caused me to feel even more isolated, but I was anxious for the feeling to end and to be done… period. And it will, but not today or even tomorrow. I thought the grieving process started before he filed for divorce and would end when the divorce was finalized.

Instead, for two years our divorce papers were filed, but no confirmation of divorce was completed, so I walked in hope of reconciliation…and it didn't happen. Then a new wave of grief emerged, and the process seemed to start all over again; the papers arrived, and all I had to do was sign them.

It is difficult to remember that a divorce is more than the end of a marriage; it is the end of dreams, expectations, family ties, and friendships. Yes, it's very true, the two of you have built a life together, and when the separation of your life takes place, it's not just about you two, it's about the friends you gained together, businesses, property, organization, and living to accomplish a goal together with all ends.

When a husband and wife divorce, they are leaving behind their hopes and relationships, so in all reality, it is an ending. In this way, experiencing a divorce is like experiencing a death, and the process of recovery is very similar. There are many stages of Divorce/Death you'll have to experience.

Here are a few experiences someone may experience after a divorce:

Denial

It may seem odd to experience denial after a divorce; however, it does occur in strange circumstances. For instance, while calling the insurance company to confirm coverage, they ask, "Are you calling for you or your husband?" Immediately, I had to get myself together and not allow them to hear or sense me break down, or you run into someone you both know, and they ask, "How is your husband doing?" All you can do is nod and say, "Well," and I'm thinking they can see me shrinking in pain.

It is tempting not to tell the other person about the divorce, so instead, you pretend you are still together, or you just give a general response (which you can do but it might provide room for more awkward moments later). This is a form of denial.

Anger

This reaction is far more familiar leading up to the divorce; most likely, this is experienced in spades. While the name of your ex might no longer provoke an immediate angry reaction, some anger will pop up in unexpected places. Perhaps a co-worker displays the same characteristics that your ex did, a neighbor laughs like your ex, or your child looks and acts more and more like your ex every day. Unexpected anger toward the co-worker, neighbor, or child which has little to do with them and far more to do with whom they resemble becomes an anger trigger point for you.

Yes, I know the Bible says be angry but sin not. So stop, take a breather, and recognize where the anger is stemming from; doing so will prevent your anger from being projected onto an innocent target. Never allow anyone else to pay for someone else's crime or time.

Bargaining

Just when it seems like every angle has been analyzed, more uncertainty will emerge. These inquiries rehash old issues as well as new ones resulting from the divorce process. Questions like, "If only I had asked for this," "Why didn't I fight for that," "I should have spent more time," and "How come things turned out this way?" are abundant. By then, most friends and relatives are exhausted from this process and offer little answers or comfort and begin to be more and more intolerant to your emotions.

You began to text and call your ex, commit to crazy pleas or promises of change, but it's all emotions and egos. The reality of your pain now begins with I want you to feel the pain I feel, especially if your ex-spouse refuses to communicate with you. It angers you but the reality is they are in pain as well; they just display it differently than you do.

Depression

No matter how the divorce happens it was and is a divorce. Going through the holidays without your ex and the routine and traditions that you developed will be difficult. I expected to feel even more depressed between Thanksgiving and New Year's Day as this is a time of intense celebration, family activities, and getting together with family and friends, and our home was the headquarters.

When feeling the height of the depression, this is when I thought he was doing perfectly fine without me. The truth was, our struggle and emotions surrounding the divorce were processed differently. I had to stop sitting at home thinking about last year at my ex's family's house and the good time I had. Instead, I had to start new traditions that I had always wanted to try, such as going out of the country for Christmas or feeding the homeless on Thanksgiving.

Acceptance

At the end of a long cycle of emotions, acceptance will be reached. It is more comfortable talking about the end of the marriage without extraneous or bitter feelings. Acceptance is similar to the death of a close family member; this process will take years to finally achieve. Your children, on the other hand, will not be on the same schedule as they will look like they have accepted it far sooner, but a couple of years later they will show signs of anger, depression, resentment, and ultimately one of the parents will be the target of their anger and disappointment.

Don't be surprised by this, but expect it and anticipate getting them professional help, and get yourself some help too. There is nothing wrong with a counselor, psychiatrist, or a psychologist because they can help you navigate to a healthy mind and heart by releasing your thoughts in a pure and honest conversation.

My testimony...

I did not get married desiring to go through a divorce. I learned that divorce is hard, painful, and demands time for proper healing. By having a better understanding of my emotions and viewing divorce in the same light as a death, it helped me to glide through the stages, instead of stumbling in the dark and self-destructing.

When I first got married, my husband was my knight in shining armor. He took me from a life of pain and disappointment, but he was unaware that the pain I felt would be his uphill battle. Now, he has married a woman without a true identity and who also wants to recreate a life without accepting or understanding why she wanted it. I was married at 18, and I lived day to day as if I was ok.

Depression was a constant struggle, and insecurities were a blanket of warmth. Lies were the only real communication because heck, why should I let him see the mess he inherited? Having our children were the happiest times in our life. Church and ministry became the shadow of dealing with our marriage. Staying busy in the church made us feel like we were contributing to our marriage, but the reality was, we were avoiding our marriage.

I remember one day later on in our marriage my husband said to me, *"You have a human void that I could never fulfill,"* but in my mind, I was saying, "Just try, just do it." However, it wasn't a void for him or anyone else to fulfill; I truly needed God.

We survived for 24 years, and just a few months away from our 25th wedding anniversary, my husband decided with all other circumstances presented that he no longer loved me or wanted to battle. At first, anger set in because he sang a song for years… *till death do us part.* He didn't lie; every lyric he sang was the truth, because as I look back, Annetta had to die, so she could live.

Do I believe he loved me? Yes, now I do, but the pain made me not accept his love.

Do I believe we could have made it? Yes, but the hurt, pain, words, and actions that occurred made it difficult to connect or reconnect.

The truth is learning how to be honest and transparent to the person you decide to live your life with.

How did a divorce affect me emotionally and physically? My marriage housed a lot of mental, verbal, emotional, and physical abuse, which began to set me deeper into a dark place. The divorce killed my ability to understand the true meaning of healthy love and communication.

Unhappiness

Divorced people have worse physical and mental health compared to married adults. Divorced adults on average are less happy if they haven't faced the truth and forgiven.

Depression

Divorced individuals, particularly women, are more vulnerable to depression. We give of ourselves to the point of not having ourselves to give. Giving is the nurturing part of our lives, but it can also play a big part in our own sadness, if there is no balance.

Divorced women have higher levels of stress, lower levels of psychological well being, and poorer self-esteem.

False intimacy

Some divorced women and men (especially) substitute casual sex for closeness and intimacy. This may eventually produce greater feelings of loneliness, unhappiness, and lower self-esteem and can even lead to substance abuse.

Substance abuse

Divorced adults, especially men, drink more alcohol than married adults, putting them at risk for addiction (I began to drink and party because I wanted to fill a void, again).

HURT PEOPLE HURT PEOPLE

"The greatest thing about after a divorce is the healing and accepting your fault, asking for forgiveness, and beginning to live your life with hope for the better." -Annetta M. Williams

How do you begin to build healthy communication after divorce?

_____

_____

_____

How do you prepare your mind to live after divorce?

_____

_____

_____

How do you feel about you after divorce?

_____

_____

_____

Chapter Four

A Godly Woman with a Purpose

"And we know that all things work together for good to them that love God, to them who are called according to His purpose." Roman 8:28

What are the characteristics of a Godly woman with a purpose?

A Godly woman with a purpose has an inner strength to overcome inner demons and conflicts.

A Godly woman with a purpose has the personal strength to succeed in the world and focus on her Godly success.

A Godly woman with a purpose will not have an impact on her immediate surroundings until she conquers those inner hindrances that prevent her from knowing God.

A Godly woman with a purpose must be committed and allow God's desires to become her desires.

A Godly woman with a purpose must carry and share the wisdom that she seeks from God in all things.

A Godly woman with a purpose carries in her spirit, *"I can do all things through Christ which strengtheneth me."* Philippians 4:13

A Godly woman with a purpose gets her strength from the Lord. *"But they that wait upon the Lord shall renew their strength; they shall mount up with wings as eagles; they shall run, and not be weary; and they shall walk, and not faint."* Isaiah 40:31

With so many different situations in life, it's very easy to get distracted. But when you know that you can find peace in God's will, you'll begin to think in the spiritual realm instead of the physical realm. As today's women, we come face to face with many obstacles, yet our assurance comes from above. Many women are stagnated in a place of trying to figure out their purpose. Listen, stop trying to figure it out, and allow God to give you a purpose.

One of the best instructional guides for defining a woman's purpose is located inside the Holy Bible in Proverbs 31. One day as I read Proverbs 31, I realized that I didn't understand what I was reading, nor was I ready to conform to it. Yet I comprehended that all I had to do was follow the lead of the scriptures, and all he had to do was appreciate me. Still, my first thoughts were, "No way, I know there has to be more for the man to do."
After my second attempt at reading Proverbs 31, I said to myself, "Well, if I do this, I will reap my rewards." I began my search, but what rewards was I searching for?
Upon the third time of reading Proverbs 31, I found myself in a desperate state.

I was going through some things in my marriage, so I needed a Word to help get me over. But this time, I heard God speak these words to me: "No, go to Proverbs 14:1."

Every wise woman buildeth her house: but the foolish plucketh it down with her hands. After the LORD led me to Proverbs 14:1, He spoke these words, *"I turned you around for my purpose, and you don't see what I have done for you all these years. I want to shape you for my purpose."*

I was amazed by how God's Word spoke directly to my heart. His Word allowed me to know the difference between a wise and foolish woman. As I read Proverbs 31 for the fourth time, it became clearer. At last, I understood that God has a defined plan for a woman to be a nurturer, to build our homes, and for our homes to be sanctified places of praise, solely for our families and us. After reading Proverbs 31, I felt empowered, and I wanted to share my experience with everyone about the true glory in becoming a virtuous woman.

No longer was I afraid of the role or responsibilities that came along with being a virtuous woman. Finally, I was in a position to embrace my promises…promises that were secretly hidden in the role of the Proverbs 31 woman.

My Afterthoughts...

Have you ever felt like the Lord is taking a concept or principle and repeatedly placing it before you? I've learned that when I sense this, it's to my benefit and for His glory that I pay close attention.

Oftentimes, I have no idea as to "Why?" God has chosen to impress upon my heart this particular subject. Still, my past experiences have taught me that I must listen to God; besides, my desires changed as my situation changed, which allowed my desires to become God's desires. With that being said, the favor of the Lord rode on my back in every endeavor I put my hands out to do.

Proverbs 31:30 says, *"Favour is deceitful, and beauty is vain but a woman that feareth the Lord, she shall be praised."* In order to be a godly woman, first and foremost, God MUST be at the center of all you think, say, and do. This transformation can only take place when God's Word has been deeply rooted in your heart, which spills over into your belly and formulates out of your mouth. Meaning, you have to live, eat, sleep, and drink the Word on a daily basis.

Listen, beautiful. Yes, it gets hard sometimes to try and stay focused, but it's much easier to follow directions than to create self-destruction for your life. I recall a time when I was praying about something specific in my marriage and I asked God to please show my husband what he needed to do, and the Lord replied, *"Be concerned about your own roles, and leave his alone. I have given you both simple details and responsibilities, but you're so focused on what he's not doing that you don't even know your role."*

At that very moment, I realized how we needed to learn how to communicate in prayer. On that day, my prayers changed, all because God scolded me to step into my position. A position to do only what I'm called to do and nothing else, a position that would be a benefit to my husband and not a curse.

There are many questions that you can ask yourself when defining your purpose.
Have you ever asked yourself, "What is my purpose in life?" You aren't alone. Many people go through life feeling discouraged about themselves and thinking they don't have a purpose in life. But that's not true. Whoever you are, whatever your life experiences, talents, physical ability, or role…you have a purpose. The one thing you must do is narrow down in prayer for your purpose and ask for the direction of your journey which leads you to your purpose.

It's within my reflections of life experiences and obstacles; I had to realize that purpose sometimes brings pain, but the pain didn't eliminate my purpose.

"For we are God's workmanship, created in Christ Jesus to do good works, which God prepared in advance for us to do."
- Ephesians 2:10

Here are a few things I need you to keep in mind:

- » God created me!
- » I am not an accident or a by the way!
- » God has a plan for me!
- » I have a purpose in life!

Many times, as women we look for approval based on our outer appearance, so we wear weave, wigs, makeup, or some get surgery just for the approval of another flawed individual. Instead, let's focus on our character and the heart of all matters, which is a fingerprint of our purpose. When I think of flaws, I don't think of looks, hair, makeup, or scars, or a lack of beauty as folks say.

Flaws are the lack of love for oneself and others.

Flaws are the inability to see the greatness in yourself (purpose).

Flaws are not recognizing the One who directs your life…God.

After my sickness and treatments, I lost my hair, and it never grew back. If I would have focused on my hair, I would've missed my purpose of my being alive and living again. At that point I didn't assume I was flawed; instead, I began to tell myself that God is allowing me to embrace the inner beauty and to walk in my outer beauty.

My outer beauty is living for God while serving Him and serving others. While walking this journey it requires me to have faith in Him and confidence in myself. This is how certain circumstances in my life became the push to pursue my purpose unapologetically. Listen, my troubles turned out for the best because they forced me to learn from the textbook (Bible).

"Truth from your mouth means more to me than striking it rich in a gold mine." Psalm 119:71-72

A Godly Woman with A Purpose

"We can't keep getting distracted by the things that don't define our purpose. Knowing who God is will place you in a position of knowing who you are and help identify your purpose.

Life is a series of problem-solving opportunities. The problems you face will either defeat you or develop you—depending on how you respond to them." –Annetta M. Williams

Do you know your Purpose in life?

_____

_____

_____

How do I embrace my Purpose?

_____

_____

_____

What can I do right now to move forward in my purpose?

_____

_____

_____

Chapter Five

A Godly Woman

"God is in the midst of her; she shall not be moved:"
- Psalm 46:5

Many have gotten the term *"Godly Woman"* twisted. When they hear those words, it automatically draws them to think of Proverbs 31, a chapter that is assumed to be written for married women only, but that's far from the truth. A Godly Woman has godly characteristics and a godly attitude that she must live and display daily. Yes, we all have a purpose in life. Yes, we all have greatness in our lives, but the key is, how are you handling your purpose and greatness, and is it benefiting the Kingdom of God?

"Can I live as a Godly Woman in these days?" This is a question we must all ask ourselves. Truly, a *Godly Woman* is someone who diligently strives to possess a Godlike character. No, it doesn't mean that she'll be perfect, but it does mean that she is striving for perfection in her walk and talk because she studies the Word and applies it to her life. In doing so, the attributes of God are illuminated through her, and His Light becomes a part of who she is.

A Godly Woman is a reflection of God; she is dedicated to the cause of Christ, who is willing and ready to serve and worship Him in the *beauty of holiness.*

If any of you lack wisdom, let him ask of God, that giveth to all men liberally, and upbraideth not; and it shall be given him. (James 1:5)

To obtain a working knowledge of God's character, we must spend quality time reading His Word -- The Bible.

This can be difficult for us at times I think, because some of us approach the Word as if it were a book to be read for a history class! But the bible is not just another book ... it is Jesus Himself

The Living Word for which we can live by and has all the answers to our daily life. Do you want to know how to handle your kids look in the book (Bible) you want to know how to love your spouse look in the book (Bible) you want to know how to treat your neighbor right look in the book (Bible). Yes, we fall because we're still in flesh, but our main goal is to please Christ. So don't be dismayed by the untruth of this world that says, "No man is perfect;" instead, tell them, "Yes, one Man is perfect, and His name is Jesus Christ, the Holy One whom you were created from." So, yes, perfection does reside within you.

In the Word of God, it is written in the book of Genesis about a man and woman named Adam & Eve who set the standard for us all. Eve was created from the rib of man; this, my sister, is a symbol of God's perfection. God is stating, "I already created a perfect image of me, so now I will remove part of his perfection to create another perfected image, an image that shall be called a woman from man's rib, which means when he breathes, so shall she." Now, that alone is a symbol of perfection through Jesus Christ.

Do you believe you are a Godly Woman? Read on; you will be blessed!

The idea of sustaining a Godly Woman's image through every stage of our lives challenges us even more; therefore, we must take a step outside the mindset of maintaining a relationship with God and beginning to learn God in different ways.

The key to understanding this principle is to realize that the solution in our lives is on God's terms, a principle that may take a lifetime for us to truly understand. If we want to be Proverbs 31 women, we must live on God's terms and not our own.

I recall a time when I was in my twenties, and I was just beginning to discover myself as a woman, yet I was still somewhat confused. I'm quite confident in speaking this truth: I truly did not understand God's love for me, but I had enough faith to know God exists, and His presence is real. I will never forget the time God brought the reality of His presence into my life. The man who I was physically and sexually attracted to, the man who I fell in love with and married, became the man who changed right before my eyes. He changed when he placed God on a higher standard, which made me look deeper at my own relationship with God.

Matthew 5:16, "Let your light so shine before men, that they may see your good works, and glorify your Father which is in heaven."

This scripture is exactly what my husband was doing, but I truly believe he was unaware that he was displaying the characteristics of the true and living God. In my eyes, God went for the jugular when he sent His own Son. No, He didn't deal with the issues as something remote and unimportant;

instead, God sent His Son, Jesus, to personally take on the human condition. He purposefully entered the disordered mess of a struggling humanity in order to set it right once and for all. This is what I learned from Jesus' message: Love hurts. Yes, it was a sacrifice, but it is also everlasting. Then I asked myself the question, "WHAT IS MY PURPOSE FOR LIVING?"

This simple question sparked my journey as a GWWAP. Now, I have a better understanding of my purpose, a purpose that I am sure of. A purpose where I can boldly and firmly say, "I am a Godly Woman with a Purpose." Now, you may be asking yourself, "How can I find and understand my purpose?" Well, here's the answer: Through prayer and studying the Word of God. His Word will define your plan and give you a better understanding of your purpose, so you can boldly walk in God's destiny.

God's plan is the pathway for your very existence, and your purpose is the defined duty of the work that God has planned for your life. When your destiny and purpose is being fulfilled, this, my sister, is God's Will, and this is what's pleasing in His sight.

Chapter Six

Woman build your Faith, you will overcome doubt

"That your faith should not stand in the wisdom of men, but in the power of God." 1 Corinthians 2:5

Doubt is something that exists, and at some point, we all have experienced it.

Question: Why, when bad things happen to us, we wonder why God isn't moving on our time?

Why, when our prayers aren't answered, we are quick to doubt that God can see, hear, or even care?

Why, when someone asks a question about God that you can't answer, doubt rear its ugly head?

My sister and friend, this is when we have to replace doubt with faith. But how do we overcome doubt and have faith in what we can't see? The Bible states in Hebrews 11:1, *"Faith is the substance of things hoped for and the evidence of things unseen."*

No, you can't see doubt, nor can you see faith, so why not take a chance on faith; at least it will never fail you. Doubt creates issues such as fear, anger, disappointment, envy, and many other things that do not please our Father. This is why it is important to understand what causes a Christian to doubt God. Perhaps the primary cause is Satan (Genesis 3:1-6). Just as God, Jesus, and the angels work in a spiritual realm to draw us toward heaven as our home, Satan and his demons work to drag us away from our heavenly home.

One of their weapons is to plant seeds of doubt and fear, and neither is God's creation. When we doubt the existence of God, the power of God, the love of God, or the sacrifice of Christ, we give the enemy full control of our minds. This is when he has the ability to make us question our very own existence:

Am I saved?
Does God have plans for my life?
Will I ever get married?
Will I ever have children?

Those simple questions become doubtful statements. What we speak out of our mouths can either be life or death because power is in the tongue.

Some years ago, I was told by a doctor that I would never have kids due to medical reasons. Well, I believed the doubt. I'll never forget how the devil made me believe I was less of a woman, and I was cursed by God.

I will never forget the August of 1996; I was in attendance at a revival service, and God spoke through a preacher and said, "The curse is off your womb." I thought the preacher was finished, but he continued by saying, "You blocked your wound with the spirit of doubt and not turning it over to God, and what you desire God will grant, but you must have faith." Three weeks later, I went to the doctor, and I was five weeks pregnant.

Today, I stand as a believer knowing we can cause our blessing to be held up on doubt. If you have faith, God will open your womb! By faith, He will restore your marriage, children, and ministry to flourish for his Glory!

My Afterthoughts...

Days of distress and pain don't exist. No, I'm not naïve, but it's how I respond that determines my outcome. My life, at one point, I thought was not worth living when you don't know what else to do.

- **Do you ever feel like you're going in circles and not making any progress? At least not the kind of progress you were expecting?**
- **Do you feel as if you can't hear or see the right path?**
- **Are the constant appeals of our world pulling you in a million different ways, causing you to question if you're headed in the right direction?**
- **Who am I, and why am I going through this?**

If you were like me, you have plans and dreams you want to fulfill, but numerous distractions can make you question, "Is this my plan or purpose?" Too many choices only mean you allowed too much into your ear gate. Are you facing endless interruptions in life and setbacks on every trail?

Yes, life is difficult at times, and most days it seems like you're just surviving instead of living out those dreams or accomplishing your goals.

Yes, there have been days I've felt like one foot was fixed to the floor while my other foot scurried in every direction. I expended a lot of energy and mental fatigue but went nowhere.

Can you all understand and relate to where I'm coming from? Wouldn't it be awesome to wake up every morning and be assured you're on the right path toward your goals? To know with certainty that you're headed in the right direction? To feel confident with each step, without constantly questioning yourself?

Too many times I've second-guessed a decision I was confident about. It wasn't from a lack of confidence but the openness of too many choices. I wanted desperately to follow God's will. I'll pray, but after prayer, I'll feel uncertain, not wanting to make a wrong move, so I wondered,

"Maybe this isn't what I'm supposed to be doing."
"Maybe this isn't part of God's plan for my life."
"Maybe I'm being overly emotional."

As I've wrestled with indecision and insecurity, I sought God's Word for help. A few months ago, I found a priceless nugget of truth in the Bible. It addressed my desire for guidance and showed me what to do when I needed clear directions.

King David composed these words in a beautiful Psalm; it's tucked within the pages of the Old Testament and it was for me, Annetta:

"Show me the right path, O LORD; point out the road for me to follow. Lead me by your truth and teach me, for you are the God who saves me. All day long I put my hope in you."
-Psalm 25:4-5

I must ask for what I don't see and to be shown the right path. Those words hit me like a brick. God said, *"Annetta, I got you. No worries;, even if you go this way, I can redeem you; even if you don't move, I can carry you. Even if you can't see, have faith like a mustard seed, and I'll show you."*

So please remember you are not alone. –God

Finish Strong!

"I can do all things through Christ who strengthens me."
Philippians 4:13

What do you want in your life?

_____

_____

_____

You say you want this, right? Well, prove how much. Fight for it! Earn it!

Overcoming obstacles is a big part of earning it.

There's always going to be resistance, but you have to overcome to accomplish anything positive that you want to have happen. The more tools you have to overcome these forces, the more likely you are to be able to stay in control and win.

What do you do when things have gone wrong?

_____

_____

_____

Many people are overwhelmed when things go wrong and feel like the rug has been pulled out from under them. Their emotions get the best of them, and instantly their enthusiasm for the whole project or task is gone… just like that!

Now is the time to identify with your struggle and address the struggle head-on with the determination for a solution.

Is this my problem to solve, or somebody else's?_____

Many people waste a lot of time on problems that aren't theirs to solve. If you're facing an obstacle that is keeping you from making progress, you need to do something about it. The source of that obstacle might be a problem that somebody else has to solve.

Ownership and Accountability are very important in life!

What are your strengths?

_____

_____

_____

You can leverage any of your personal strengths when trying to solve a problem, but when you're facing a specific obstacle, you will need to think about specific strengths. At that point, it will get you to handle what you know and grow from what you don't know.

More than personal traits think about resources, relationships, and networks. Think about all the strengths that you can put into play to help you recover anything or move past an obstacle.

Make a list of the most realities, accomplishments, and goals, and tackle each list with prayer and a key mindset. Philippians 4;13

What can I do right now to move forward?

_____

_____

_____

The first step in becoming great at something is getting obsessed about getting great at it. No obsession = no greatness! No passion, then-No Pursuit!

What's the next step in your plan?

_____

_____

_____

If it's not possible, what action can you take to move a little closer to your plan? If your plan has blown up, what is the next best viable alternate route can you take?

Knowing Who You Are

Words of exhortation from author Annetta M. Williams

First and foremost, you need to understand this simple rule as a Christian woman: you must know who your Heavenly Father is, who you are in Christ, and that God defines who you are. Listen, I wasn't told this truth; I had to learn the truth because I looked into everyone else's eyes, and the results were, I disappointed many people.
Secondly, you must get to God and know Him through prayer and His Word.
Thirdly, you must seek God to become intimately acquainted with Him, and as you do, you will begin to realize that the second thing is vitally important, especially in these last days. Listen closely; the devil preys on weak Christians, those who don't know who they are in Christ.

Lastly, as you read this life's lesson, I pray that the revelation of God's truth about who you are in Christ will rise in your heart. A truth that will cause you to stand firm against the devil.

The truth according to 2 Corinthians 5:17: You are a new creature in Christ Jesus from the moment you became born again. You are a brand-new person! The old man with devilish desires is dead!

The truth that 2 Corinthians 5:21 speaks of, *"You are made in the righteousness of God in Christ."* No, you are not righteous in and of yourself, because according to Isaiah 64:6, Our righteousness is as filthy rags. We traded our righteousness for His righteousness, and we are now righteous because of the shed blood of the Lord Jesus Christ.

God sees you as brand new through the blood of Jesus.

*"My Flaws are not my character;
My character is my Belief, and My Belief is My Purpose!"*

About The Author

Annetta M. William's dynamic, distinctive, and captivating voice carries the power to soothe and encourage the healing power of Jesus Christ. The Buffalo, New York native is inspired by her trails and obstacles to minister in song and preach from a place of victory, overcoming and being triumphant in the music industry from both the spiritual and secular world.

This humble Rhythm of Gospel Award winner has a true and undying passion for ministry and music. Annetta, the worshipper who desires to be a willing and workable vessel for God, lived and grew up in a very sound spiritual background.

Annetta M. Williams started her musical career with the St. Marks C.O.G.I.C., Buffalo, New York Gospel Chorus Choir, and C.O.G.I.C. Holy Conventional Choir. Her pathway of ministry began under family Supertindent James A. Kirkwood, her mother Daisy M. Kirkwood-Jackson who was the Choir Director/President, who pushed Annetta to sing beyond herself. At the age of 9, she was traveling around with her uncle and singing before he would preach, and she grew a passion to minister to people through music.

She was licensed at the age of 17 to preach and teach as an evangelist under Late Supertindent James A. Kirkwood. That is where her passion became more profound that songs had words that gave people life to increase their faith.

Since her first solo project, "Work In Progress", she has shared the stage with great gospel artists such as Pastor Shirley Caesar, Albertina Walker, Yolanda Adams, Pastor Marvin Winans, Donald Lawrence, and Pastor Jonathan Dunn, just to name a few. She has also worked with such artists as Delivered, Mt. Olive Lackawanna Choir, DaMarka Wheeler, Julius (Chozen) Spencer, and many more. She overwhelmed the music industry with "I'm Still Standing, I Survived it All" that was birthed from surviving cancer, stroke, and depression. This project changed her way of ministry and the mind to fight all battles with worship. She won three ROG Awards along with a United Kingdom tour in September 2018.

You can look to see **Annetta M. Williams** in the future with the title "author" behind her name. Annetta M. Williams exercises her gifts as a songwriter, producer, workshop facilitator, and an evangelist, and through her ministry endeavor **AMW Ministries/ AMW Music World.**

She is a mother of four children and three grandchildren and a professional in the medical field. Annetta is a faithful member of Tabernacle of Praise, Buffalo, New York, where she leads praise and worship, and she is on the Ministerial staff under Pastor Charles McCarley and Lady Rachel McCarley.

Ultimately, **Annetta M. Williams's** prayer is that she would be used as a vessel of change, that her spirit-filled singing and preaching will touch the lives of many, and souls will be saved throughout the United States and foreign lands. But most of all, hearing the words from God, *"Well done my good and faithful servant."*

Notes

www.ingramcontent.com/pod-product-compliance
Lightning Source LLC
Chambersburg PA
CBHW041130110526
44592CB00020B/2753